The Wind Never Stops
is dedicated to
All who are suffering on our planet.

The Wind Never Stops

A Volume of Zen Poetry

By

World Shim Gum Do
Founding Master
Zen Master Chang Sik Kim

Edited by
World Shim Gum Do Head Master
Mary Jeanette Stackhouse Kim, Ph.D.

The Wind Never Stops
Copyright © 2002 by Zen Master Chang Sik Kim

ISBN 0-9676479-4-0

Published by
World Shim Gum Do Association, Inc.
203 Chestnut Hill Avenue
Brighton, Massachusetts 02135
United States of American
www.shimgumdo.org

Library of Congress Control Number:
2002096341

The Wind Never Stops
Table of Contents

Introduction

This is Zen Master Chang Sik Kim's sixth volume of poetry. It is an assortment of poems that were written during 2001 and 2002.

Zen Master Chang Sik Kim was born in 1944 in a small farming village in South Korea. His formal academic education consisted of only three years of elementary school. When he was 13, he entered the Hwa Gye Sa Zen Temple in Seoul and studied under Zen Master Seung Sahn Lee. When Zen Master Kim was 21, his teacher sent him to undergo a 100 day retreat to try to get enlightenment. During this retreat, martial art forms were revealed to Zen Master Kim through his meditation. At one point during his retreat, Zen Master Kim had a spiritual awakening and he truly understood the power of the mind attaining Mind Sword enlightenment. Following his 100 day retreat, Zen Master Kim returned to his temple to show his new art which he called Shim Gum Do – the Mind Sword Path. The art of Shim Gum Do is an intricate martial art system including Sword, Shin Boep (Shin Boep translates to mean Body Dharma, It is a weaponless art.), Ho Shin Sul (Ho Shin Sul translates to mean self defense. It is a system of breaking holds, joint locking and pressure points.), Long Stick, Two Sword and Short Stick – about 1,000 forms in all. Zen Master Kim's enlightenment placed him as the 79th Patriarch of his Dharma lineage which began with Buddha, and passed through Bodhidharma, who was the Buddhist monk who brought Buddhism from India into China. Through meditation Bodhidharma also discovered martial art forms. These discoveries became part of the practices of the Shaolin Temple which Bodhidharma established in China. Zen Master Chang Sik Kim's discovery of Shim Gum Do revives the tradition of bringing Zen and martial arts, together.

On October 10, 1971 Zen Master Chang Sik Kim formally presented Shim Gum Do in a ceremony making the following statement: "In this degenerate age the demon is strong and the Dharma is weak. Attached to machine technology, we lose our true self, lose the true way and cannot find true life and true direction of consciousness. This world is full of suffering, complications and fighting amongst us. Soon humanity will disappear by itself. Unable to witness this suffering, we rise up with vigor, establish Shim Gum Do and use the Buddha's Great Vow of Great Love and Great Compassion." He began teaching Shim Gum Do establishing the Korean Shim Gum Do Association. In 1974, Zen Master Kim came to the United States and began teaching Shim Gum Do. In 1978 he established the American Buddhist Shim Gum Do Association and in 1991 the World Shim Gum Do Association. In 1981, Zen Master Kim established Shim Gwang Sa, The Mind Light Temple in Boston, Massachusetts. Shim Gwang Sa is the main temple of the American Buddhist Shim Gum Do Association and the World Shim Gum Do Association.

The essence of Shim Gum Do is to develop a clear mind, clear thinking and clear action through learning, studying and practicing Shim Gum Do. This process allows one to 'cut thinking'. Cutting thoughts brings one closer to understanding their truth nature, their original being that existed before our thinking process 'made' so much. The goal is to get to the core, to get to the source, to get to the heart. At that place, there is true emptiness. There are no thoughts, attachments, opinions, desires, or ego; it is a place of no hindrance. Attaining enlightenment is not about catching a fleeting vision of this state, but of entering this place, transcending time and space. The poems in this volume came through Zen Master Kim and appeared. They are not written through a process of thinking, they arise spontaneously in the moment. Zen Master Kim has said that when he picks a subject, his mind goes deeply into the subject and then he writes what he experienced there.

Zen Master Kim's poems are very diverse. They tell stories. They paint masterpieces in your imagination. They teach you about universal energy and show just how real this energy is in our everyday lives, even in as simple an action as drinking a cup of coffee. The poems show how humans are of nature and also they show the humanity of nature. They show how all things in the universe are interconnected. They give life to inanimate objects. The plates and cups in your kitchen watch you when they are awake and dream when they are asleep. The gossip you talk about at the hairdresser's forms an energy that reaches out and permeates the neighborhood. They are Zen koans, riddles designed to wake you up. They are a format to teach one about Zen and getting enlightenment.

Zen Master Kim is a member of the Korean P.E.N. Center and also a member of International P.E.N. In addition to writing poetry, Zen Master Kim is also a calligraphy brush artist, another extension of his expression. Traditionally Zen arts are teaching tools. To see the power of a calligraphy painting or to understand the meaning of a Zen poem can open your mind. Currently, Zen Master Chang Sik Kim resides and teaches Shim Gum Do at his temple. He has completed ten years of a personal retreat which includes training Shim Gum Do, everyday. During the past ten years, he hasn't missed a single day and his retreat continues. To date, Zen Master Chang Sik Kim has written more than 8,000 poems.

Through daily training at the Shim Gwang Sa Temple, students try to open their mind, become clear and recognize their original nature. For more information about Zen Master Kim's other publications or for information about Shim Gum Do, contact:

World Shim Gum Do Association
203 Chestnut Hill Avenue
Brighton, Massachusetts 02135
(617) 787-1506
www.shimgumdo.org

Mary Jeanette Stackhouse Kim, Ph.D.
Shim Gwang Sa Abbot
World Shim Gum Do Head Master
October, 2002

The Wind Never Stops

A Volume
of Zen Poetry

The Wind Never Stops

The wind never stops anywhere or any place.
The wind's heart is strong, like Rambo.
Moving at 1,000 miles an hour,
    our planet makes wind;
    it never stops.
The constant wind makes the silver and gold colors
    of the stars keep running to our planet;
    they never stop.
The continuous wind makes the lives of all
    the people, animals, fish, birds, and
    the members of the plant kingdom,
    come and go;
    their world never stops.
If the wind could stop for a moment,
    it would see its own face
    through the blue sky mirror.
If people could stop for a moment,
    their mind mirror would show them
    who they are;
    that would be great.
Stopping for a moment is very important,
You can see through to what is great and
    what is not great.
The wind never stops,
Where does the wind hide its wisdom?
If anyone knows that point,
    they can pick up the mirror
    and show our planet opening brightly,
    everywhere;
All the world's people would understand each other,
Create love and compassion for each other;
That would be great world peace.
Then, show that to the wind

and it would stop for a moment,
The wind could then see its own face;
Then the wind would understand
   to go to the places of good
   and not to go to the places of evil.

The Devil's Evil Plan

The Devil sows its evil dream in the minds
  of the world's people.
Hatred of each other, jealousy of each other,
  murder of each other and stealing from
  each other are all over,
  everywhere, on our planet;
That is all controlled by the Devil.
Look into history,
Damage has been done all over the world,
  between nations and between races,
They have had their own desires,
That makes it difficult for world peace.
That is the Devil's evil game.
Throughout our planet's history, stories
  of the hatreds, jealousies, murders, thefts
  and worse horrors have been propagated
  through storytelling acted out in theatres;
  written in books, magazines and newspapers;
  shown in movies and on television;
  and broadcast across the airwaves.
It is the Devil who is behind the creation
  of all the stories, wielding his evil plan.
Throughout history the Devil has collected
  and enjoyed all the stories.
The information gives new ideas to the Devil.
The Devil continuously makes new plans,
The new evil ideas are worse
  than the stories from before,
The Devil wants to make all kinds of prizes
  for the worse, most heinous, most evil,
The Devil enjoys more and more
  and gets stronger and stronger
  as the stories are worse and worse.

The world keeps on going and going,
The Devil brings out greater and greater evil.
More countries and more countries make war,
    they never stop.
The Devil hates one point.
Whoever has a clear mind, whoever has
    clear thinking, whoever has clear action,
    makes good dreaming for the future,
Stories of neighborhoods and countries
    helping each other appear in the world.
The Devil hates those kinds of stories,
They make the Devil want to run away.
Cover up the evil stories of the past,
    present and future,
The Devil will not get any news,
    no new stories to enjoy,
The Devil won't have any new ideas for his evil plan,
Tell more stories of good in theatres, books,
    magazines, newspapers, movies, television
    and on the radio,
Tell stories that teach people how to live,
    how to love, how to have compassion,
    how to help each other,
That is the true, great prize.
Announce all over the world, that the Devil
    and its evil have no place to enjoy in this world,
The Devil's evil plan
    cannot make any more suffering,
The Devil rolls up his dream and runs away.
The Devil's footprints disappear completely,
That makes world peace,
That is the same as peace in heaven.
Our planet dreams, for the Devil
    to never return, again.

Why is the World Suffering Now?

Look, breathe, eat, listen;
Everything you want is from desire.
You never believe others,
You steal,
You never listen,
You are not balanced,
You live by your own way.
You hate, are jealous,
You betray,
You harm others.
The rich want to be richer,
The poor become poorer.
The world is suffering,
It cannot fix itself.
The bridge never ends,
The bridge doesn't want any suffering
     to come through,
The bridge has to wait, the bridge suffers.
The bridge wants those who help each other,
     love each other,
     and are compassionate to each other,
That is the correct way for people to live their lives.
That is the way the bridge wants to be born into,
That is the way the bridge wants to live.
Whoever has eyes, nose, mouth, ears,
     hands and feet, makes their mind and thinking,
     clear and bright.
Don't hurt each other,
Live correctly,
Heaven wants that way,
The blue sky always makes a mirror
     that shows everybody,
The sound of the clear wind and

the clear air announce that they never lie.
The clear water never asks to be paid back,
It helps whoever is thirsty.
The grains, vegetables and fruit feeds the hungry,
Their sweetness never lies.
The world's suffering can be fixed,
The blue sky mirror, the sound of the wind,
    the water, the grains, the vegetables and the fruit
    tell you to learn about love and
    compassion from them,
Suffering will stop, and never happen again.

Autumn

Look at the tree, its leaves are falling down.
Fall never lies,
Fall makes the blue sky clear.
If you are truthful, try to get enlightenment.
Why are you afraid to dance like the fall leaves?
You try to get enlightenment,
    throw away like and dislike,
Look very carefully at that which is thirsty
    and that which is hungry,
At that moment, enlightenment energy appears
    like the clear blue sky.

Looking at the Flower

Look at the flower.
The ears listen,
They try to show the flower,
The eyes wake up.
The ears push and thinking, about the flower,
    appears.
The flower's perfume meets the mind,
They help each other.
The flower's seeds get enlightenment
    and each one pops out.
That sound makes the dirt and sky wake up.
Each of the flower's roots kiss the water ball,
That makes the dirt in the ground clear.
No damage is done, nobody can argue about it.
At that point, Buddha comes and goes,
Buddha's shadow dances forever.

The Rice Fiber and the Water

A rice fiber appears and lands on the water.
The water wants to live,
Its neck hangs from the rice fiber.
The rice fiber wants to teach the water,
It grabs a cloud in the blue sky and squeezes it.
The cloud's tears drop.
The water understands what a cloud is,
It understands not to hang onto the rice fiber.
The water carries and the rice fiber floats away.

Thinking Pinches

Thinking, pinching vibration
    appears throughout the body like an ocean.
The mind is lonely and chilly.
Day by day, the days push each other,
The days get squeezed between
    the body's ocean vibrations.
The thinking pinch hides a sharp blade.
All of that is the mind's shadow.
The mind is alone,
The mind pushes the shadow away.

The Wind Blows

The wind blows,
The flower's leaves dance,
They dance with the flower's perfume.
The seeds are pregnant with the wind.
The seeds give birth
    and swallow the earth's fragrance.
The flower's roots taste water,
The water blows
    and the flower's leaves appear perfectly.
Someone gets enlightenment,
How can you measure that point?
The blue sky understands that point;
The blue sky never opens its mouth;
The blue sky only shows its face,
It is, just blue.

The Bees

The bees' flying technique is so fast.
The flowers' pollen loves the bees and follows them.
The pollen makes honey,
It is sticky and sweet,
It builds up love and compassion.
The honey's face shines like a pearl.
In the honey, the faces of the pollen
    shine like dew drops.
Each season appears and disappears,
The flowers put their homeland
    into the four seasons.
The flowers complete the bees'
    leftover, unfinished dreams.
The bees' eyes wake up,
The bees work hard again.
The flowers' pollen shouts into the wind.
The bee hives line up
    with pollen make-up on their faces.
The meadow turns and wakes up.
The grass and trees are all scared,
Their faces are green.

The Thinking War

A body's lifetime is a war with thinking.
The hair turns all white.
The teeth don't understand what is going on,
    they run away,
Only the gums are left, their face is all red.
Brown patches appear on the backs of the hands.
The face wrinkles with many valleys.
Thinking is tired, in a moment it stops.
The body is exhausted, it cannot control its balance.
When will a clear mind appear?
The mirror is waiting for the mind,
The mirror is lonely.

Sickness

You say you understand, or,
  you say you don't understand,
That is a sickness.
There is no medicine for that point.
The grass and trees are all shocked,
Their faces are white.
You understand, you don't understand;
You open your mouth.
A stroke hits you like a stick,
  it wants to teach you.
Anybody who tastes water,
  never says what water tastes like,
The throat and the water understand
  what the true taste is.

The Eyes

The eyes open,
In front of the eyes,
    the sky and the earth cannot move.
The eyes close,
Darkness opens its eyes.
Thinking appears everywhere
    just like tiny, small sesame seeds.
The small thoughts tumble and tumble
    inside the brain and in the chest,
The brain and chest shake.
The small thoughts try to stop the moment.
Sleeping appears, picks up the sky and earth,
    and drops them,
That is all a dream.
Nobody can stop the dreaming.
Inside the eyes and outside the eyes,
    the mind is empty,
It holds onto the memory mirror.
In the mind,
    all the colors make a flag appear.

The Red Light

The mind turns on the red light.
Thinking cannot stop,
It comes and goes like a mouse.
The mind gives thinking a traffic ticket.
Thinking runs away,
   everywhere,
    making damage.
Thinking cannot pay the ticket.
One thought holds onto the ticket,
Thinking stops.
All kinds of thinking comes through,
They all hold onto the ticket,
They cannot pay.
They all cry.
The mind's red light is shocked,
It faints.

The Baby is Sleeping

The baby is sleeping,
Sometimes the baby smiles,
What is the baby dreaming now?
Smiling appears on the baby's face
    and then crying appears on the baby's face.
The baby wakes up,
The baby cannot talk.
The mother doesn't understand
    what dream the baby had.
The mother's thinking is confused.
A bigger baby understands the little baby's
    dreaming.
The little baby plays for a little while,
The baby sleeps and dreams again.
The baby's dreaming and the baby's thinking
    are so clear.
The baby's mind,
    sleeping or not,
    is always the same.
The mother's breast never lies to the baby.

The Blind

There is sound,
The ear listens, clearly.
The thoughts are always talking.
The mind tries to understand the sound,
the listening ear and,
the thoughts,
At that moment the mind is blind.

Life is Everything, Everything is Life

Life is everyday movement.
People love each other, they hate each other.
They are so wild, the houses are too small.
Close, faraway, in the four different directions,
Everywhere, it is so crowded,
    everyone bumps into each other.
A person's life is so noisy.
The movement of everyday life
    is just like the flapping of wings.
Everybody carries their own dreams,
They work hard,
The leftover shade is lonely.
The shade cannot live in the day, in the night
    or in the wind.
The moment life looks back,
The shade carries a flag
    and plants it in the ground.
The shade opens its eyes only one time,
They never close.

Desire

The desire of each single person, the group
    and the whole country makes trouble.
People grab their desire,
    and make their own prominence.
After the moment passes, they understand
    their desire wasn't correct.
The water and the air don't have desire,
They can go wherever they want.
The water and air visit everywhere
    and show love and compassion.
The grass and trees don't make much desire,
They only desire enough to live and enjoy.
The stone shoots out.
The stone cannot even make thoughts about desire.
The stone lives forever.
The stone teaches how to be eminent.
People have eyes and ears,
    they cannot see correctly or hear correctly.
Life and death make heaven and hell.
Life and death want to teach those
    who don't see correctly
    and those who don't hear correctly.

Breathing

Breathe correctly and clearly.
In one breath, 10,000 thoughts appear
    and disappear.
Unlike people, the grass and trees breath one time,
    and they carry the whole mountain.
Thinking tries to get enlightenment,
Thinking looks for the mind.
The clear mind is never shocked,
The clear mind never moves.

The Earth's Breath

The potato's mouth and the sweet potato's mouth
　　hold onto the earth's breath.
The taste and the smell of the potato
　　and the sweet potato are different.
Look inside the two potatoes,
Their color is different.
Take one bite of each,
Inside the mouth the potatoes
　　are introduced to the teeth.
The tongue understands the potato
　　and the sweet potato.
The potato and the sweet potato
　　completely give themselves to the tongue.
The teeth, tongue and the potatoes
　　dance around inside the mouth.
The potato and sweet potato make peace
　　with the hunger damage in the stomach.

The Fingertips and the Tips of the Toes

The fingertips touch everything,
    and the tips of the toes dream about all of it.
Everything appears to the tips of the toes,
The fingertips dance beautifully.
The fingertips and the tips of the toes
    are very quiet now.
During the night, under the blanket,
    they talk to each other.
Their stories go into the darkness of the night,
    everywhere.
That makes the body dream perfectly.

Thinking's Tail

Thinking goes millions and millions
    of miles far away.
Thinking's tail cannot jump over the mind.
The action of thinking's end point
    draws a mountain.
Action and thinking chase each other
    and hide from each other,
On the way, dreaming is always with them,
    it never changes,
Action and thinking never know
    the dreaming is there.

Understand

In the mountain temple
    the monks are in meditation.
Finally the monks understand the point.
The monks want to sell what they finally understand
    to the mirror.
The mirror looks and takes what the monks
    understood.
The monks wonder how to make a technique
    for the mirror to understand itself,
They have no idea.
At that moment the mirror calls the day and night.
The mirror yells to the day and nigh
    not to brag about themselves.
The day and night are very quiet,
They learned that from the mirror.
The day and the night go back to their own way.

Hitting the Chest

Open the newspaper,
Every truth comes through.
The stories come from every community
    in the world.
The newspapers spread the stories out
    all over the whole world.
The radio and television are shocked,
    and they wake up.
The newspaper stories keep going day and night,
The stories cut through the eyes and ears.
The stories hit every person's chest
    and vibrate forever.

The Rifle and the Sword

The hands of the army soldiers
    hold a rifle and a sword.
The army fires their rifles.
Whom does the firing help?
The soldiers' fingertips control life and death.
The soldiers and their enemies look at each other
    and hold their breaths.
They fire at each other,
They all die.
After death, all of the soldiers' faces are measured.
They can't argue anymore,
It is nobody's fault.
The injuries leave the bodies of the soldiers,
Finally free of pain,
The injuries jump on the scale and dance.

The Spring Flower Cuts Through the Mountain

The spring flower cuts through the mountain.
That technique is secret.
The technique is practiced during the winter.
That technique excites the spring wind.
The spring rain visits softly.
The spring rain looks for the secret technique,
It doesn't want the clouds to know.
In the Spring the mountain's chest warms up,
It wants to hide the spring flowers.
The mountain gets rid of its shadow.

The Office

In the office, the telephone sits on a desk.
The telephone rings, rings and shouts.
The white paper looks around for a pen.
A cup of coffee sits in front of the paper.
The cup of coffee teases the secretary's hands.
The hands make a mistake
    pushing the coffee cup away.
The cup falls on the desk,
The coffee pours out of the cup,
It sounds like it's crying.
The coffee spreads out like a river to the ocean.
The office is busy all day long.
The office kicks all the workers out.
The office wants to dream during the night.

The Hairdresser's

At the hairdresser's, the women talk to each other.
The stories wake up the neighborhood.
The stories point everywhere.
The mirror looks at the women
    and makes their smiles show up.
The mirror grabs the women's hair and shakes it.
The stories fall out and drop down.
The women's thoughts tumble onto the floor.
On the floor,
    their fallen hair holds on to their thoughts,
The women's hair is scared,
    it turns black.

The Rabbit on the Mountain

On the mountain there is one rabbit.
It makes the mountain clear.
The rabbit runs and sends the small rocks rolling.
The tumbling stones warm the mountain.
The mountain rabbit keeps hopping,
Each footprint turns into a rabbit,
Each footstep makes all kinds of colors appear.
The mountain rabbit never counts
    today and tomorrow,
That is the mountain rabbit's wisdom.
That wisdom always makes the mountain grow up.

The Mind

You have a mind.
The mind looks for the mind,
That is stupid.
The mind looks at the hands and feet,
The hands and feet are always alive.
Each technique appears,
In each technique,
    the mind makes a flower.

The Sun

The east sun is a circle.
The west sun is a circle.
The sun's beginning and end
    never change.
That is why the truth dances.
The blue sky's smile is always blue.

The Mind's Name

'Mind' is a name,
That is not the true mind.
A 'name' is not the truth.
What is the truth?
You cannot add or take away,
That is the truth.
The mind is not like the airspace,
The mind is not like the universe,
The universe is not empty.
Water doesn't understand that it is water.
Water naturally follows its way.
Wherever water goes,
    it shows life and death clearly.
The mind tastes water, the mind is clear like water.
The mind understands how to measure in front
    and behind, clearly.

The Mind and Thinking

The mind can kill thinking,
The mind can give thinking life;
That is the mind's way.
The metal dragon can eat metal and live,
That is the metal dragon's way.
The stone tiger makes the stone beautiful
    and makes the mountain great,
That is the stone tiger's way.
The metal dragon can eat the lightning barbecue,
That makes the clouds appear, beautifully.
The mind makes a flower and perfume appears.

The Nighttime Snow Fallen Path

The snow falls on the foot path during the night.
The snow's face appears clearly, white.
It carries what looks like a clear mind.
The path is slippery.
Thinking skis across the snow.
Walking, very carefully, makes footprints
    in the snow.
The wind comes, rolls the snow up and runs away.
In the night, the guests put on their winter coats.
Snow falls on the way,
The footprints talk to each other.
The dark night is in the snow, hiding, it dreams.
Winter fans the snow, and makes it dance.
Midnight wakes up the strongest cold general,
The road on the mountain
    looks like a white snow ocean.

One Picture

The moment grabs the mountain and the river
    in one picture.
In that picture, the mountain and the river
    look as though they are being penalized.
All the faces of nature appear in the picture.
The pen's brush cannot copy that picture.
The camera's shot collects all the minds.
In the picture, all the people are lined up;
Thinking cannot move.

You Cannot Lie

The picture cannot lie.
The picture grabs the mind, the thinking
    and the body,
    and presents them.
Everybody believes that picture.
In that picture Buddha cannot lie
    to his original face.

The Angel's Secret

The Angel's secret is afraid of the picture.
The picture grabs the Angel's secret,
The picture keeps going for trillions of years,
The Angel's secret never sleeps and never complains.
The strongest person and
    the most knowledgeable person
    in the earth and sky
    compete for that picture.
They can never attain the Angel's secret.

Silence is a Great Teacher

In the one picture, silence introduces you and me.
The grass and the trees jump into the picture
    and are introduced to the four seasons.
The teacher and the students jump into the picture
    and announce themselves.
The parents and the children jump into the picture
    and show who they are.
Heaven and Hell learn from
    the one picture's silence.

Lifetime Meditation

Meditate for a lifetime,
Try to get enlightenment,
Where is it?
You want something,
Great or not,
Is that a mistake or stupid?
Grab everything,
Let them go to their original point.
That is greatness.
So,
Even if one piece of dust jumps into the mind,
You cannot take it away.
However,
Have or not have,
What is true emptiness?
These are all techniques made by thinking,
That is why all kinds of thoughts grow bigger,
Eventually becoming like dead trees, they rot.
If you understand one piece of dust and one splinter,
You can understand life and death.
The handle of enlightenment never perishes,
It opens wisdom,
Its sharp movement cuts through the moment.
Moment by moment meditation is empty,
Everything is let go to their original point.
That is the beginning of enlightenment's door.

You Cannot Pass Over Wisdom

The green mountain never passes over the blue sky.
In the mountain, the stream water never looks back
    to its source.
The river never fusses at the stream.
The ocean understands what is going on.
The ocean never passes over wisdom,
It is always dancing.

One Drink

One drink, and happiness and sadness appear
    and tumble inside the chest.
In front of the eyes, the big face
    and the scary face float.
One moment singing, one moment crying,
One moment singing, one moment crying.
Shout one word!
The night is quiet and scared.
History can always change,
The effect of one drink never changes.
One drink reads the bartender's thoughts,
One drink tells you the bartender worries
    if you can make it home.

The Mind is Hiding

Soybeans ferment and become miso and soy sauce.
Mix before thinking and after thinking,
    and they ferment, just like the soybeans.
Cut through and clear thinking appears,
Just like the blue sky mirror.
The mind is hiding,
The clear mirror doesn't make the mind shy.

The Body and the Clothes

The clothes fit the body perfectly.
The hands and feet are happy.
Each thought that appears
    makes the 10,000 thoughts dance.
Cutting one thought makes happiness,
Thinking wrestles with the mind.
The mirror is the judge,
The blue sky cannot wait to smile,
The stars' eyebrows bend, like a bow.

The Day and Night Pinch Each Other

Moment by moment the day and night
    pinch each other.
They give each other their seat.
They never talk or complain to each other.
Sir Sun, Sir Moon and the Sir Stars softly come in,
    day and night.
Day and night pinch them.
The faces of Sir Sun, Sir Moon and the Sir Stars
    are all shocked,
The all run to the mirror.

The Grass and Trees Enjoy Pinching

The grass and trees enjoy pinching each other.
The grass and trees' roots dig into the ground,
    pinching.
Their roots pinch the ground water,
The grass and trees' faces get bigger.
Any kind of bug
    that runs into the grass and the trees,
    love and enjoy pinching.
The shiny green eyes of the grass and trees open,
    day and night.

Inside the Eyes

Look into the eyes.
Inside the eyes,
    truth and enlightenment cannot lie.
The eyes open in front of the eyes.
The wind has no clothes,
    as it comes and goes
    and hangs around in front of the eyes.
Open the eye's light one more time.
Thinking follows,
At that moment, thinking stops.
The mind cannot make a baby,
It throws away its first and last name.

The Life of a Plate

Before the plate had life,
Dirt, water, fire and air came together,
   and then tumbled together
   and made a plate.
After, the plate had life,
It grabs everything and lets it go.
It works hard and kicks out the day and night.
The plate dies,
The plate runs into the ground,
The plate buries its dreams.
People follow the plate's dreams,
The plate wants to hug them.

The Plate's Face

The plate's face is a circle.
The plate's face invites
    whoever is looking for the mind.
The mind is empty,
The plate's face teaches what emptiness is.
People have so much thinking,
    they only make thinking,
    they only follow their thinking.
The plate understands that is too much thinking,
    that is not looking for the mind.
The plate grabs their mouths
    and makes them kiss the food.
The plate grabs their minds,
The plates shows them all the way around the circle,
The mind follows all the way around the plate,
The mind enjoys that.

The Plate Reads the Words

The plate reads the words.
During its lifetime,
    the plate never forgets those words.
The plate draws a picture
    of every different kind of food.
The food never leaves the plate.
On the plate the food tastes great.
The food makes the hungry wake up
    and gives them joy and happiness.
The plate never changes what it is doing.
The words and the drawings learn from the plate,
    throughout their lifetime.
They want to,
    but they can never jump off the plate.

The Plate Has One Eye

You don't understand the plate,
That is the same as not understanding who you are.
That makes the plate sad.
You say you understand the plate,
That plate teaches you who you are.
The plate opens its happiness,
The plate understands all of that
    from its own eye light.
The plate doesn't need a mouth,
The plate has only one circle.
One circle hits the sky and hits the ground,
They all enjoy each other.

The Highest Wisdom

If you can see, you can understand the plate.
That is the highest wisdom.
If you understand
    that there are all kinds of food on the plate.
That is the highest knowledge.
If you understand the plate's circle,
Your mind returns to its original point.

How Old is the Plate

The plate never counts its age.
The plate practices that way for its lifetime.
The plate never thinks,
The plate never holds a mind.
That is the plate's wisdom.
The plate has no mind,
Those who have a mind all run to the plate.
At breakfast, lunch and dinner,
They all whine for the plate.

Life and Death

Life and death appear on a face,
They are separated by a moment.
Life dies, burns out and turns into ashes.
Someone understands life and death,
After they die, they cannot open their mouth.
Coming and going, life and death make no sound.
The truth shows the way and opens the road.
The perfume of life and death understands the truth,
The perfume dances alone.

The First Day of February

The first day of February
    understands the faces of everything.
Everybody holds onto their own dreams.
They leave their homes.
Outside they run into the white snow,
The snow says a cold, "Hello!"
Their faces freeze red,
They move step by step.
Their footprints dream forward for 10,000 miles.
The white snow makes a bridge,
    and welcomes everyone.
The white snow slaps the ice in the face.

The Loan

From birth, you owe.
Your lifetime's biggest loan
    comes from your parents.
Your parents made you,
    they helped you,
    they loved you
    and they were compassionate to you,
That is what you owe your parents.
You borrowed knowledge from your teachers.
Your sisters, brothers, friends and relatives
    all helped you,
You also owe them.
Lives are lived.
Everyone helps each other and owes each other.
Before dying, how many people pay off their loans?
How many people know that they owe those
    who helped them and who taught them?
In the universe, all of nature owes each other.
Where does all this come from?
The loan is very big,
    so big.
Nobody can triumph over the loan.
Moment by moment,
    the moments help each other
    and give loans to each other;
They cannot live without borrowing and lending.
The mirror lives by borrowing
    from light and darkness.

The Mind is Free

Buddha understood borrowing and owing,
Finally he got enlightenment,
His mind was empty.
Bodhidharma paid off his loan,
All of his thoughts were thrown through his mind.
Every loan asks the eminent teachers
    to pay them back,
The eminent teachers open their eyes
    and hide their minds.
You say you don't want to borrow,
    but still you will owe, anyway.
Liking borrowing or not liking borrowing,
    no matter what,
    the loan will push you down.
If you don't owe anything,
    that is true enlightenment.
The mind is so quiet,
The mind is free of borrowing.

One Painting

One painting borrows a piece of white paper,
    a brush and black ink,
A picture is drawn and a painting appears.
The drawing lives on the paper for hundreds of years
    because it owes the paper, the brush and the ink;
It cannot leave.
The drawing cannot open its mouth.
If someone understands the story of the drawing,
They can only say "I am sorry"
They leave, but their words stay with the painting.

The Dust

The dust flies in the air and sunlight,
The dust lives on the ground.
The dust borrows from the air,
   the sunlight and the ground.
The dust passes millions and trillions of years,
The dust owes the air,
   the sunlight and the ground;
It cannot pay back.
The dust's loan builds up like a great mountain,
It cannot move.
The dust feels like a criminal,
The dust is ashamed.

The Big Tree

The big tree grows up on the biggest mountain.
As the tree lives it borrows water and dirt.
The tree drinks water,
The water is cleaned out and returned,
That water makes a river,
The river looks for the ocean.
The dirt worries that the tree won't pay it back,
That the tree will run away to the ocean.
The dirt grabs the tree,
Day and night it squeezes and squeezes the big tree.

The Worm

The worm borrows from the dirt.
Underground, the worm makes a house,
   lives and enjoys.
The dirt lends to the worm,
The dirt asks the worm to pay back.
The worm doesn't care,
Inside the ground, it makes its house everywhere.
The dirt is very worried that the worm
   will never pay back what it owes.
The dirt wants to talk to the worm,
It looks very carefully,
It sees that the worm doesn't have any ears,
The dirt understands that the worm cannot hear.
The dirt invites the wind,
The wind teases the worm.
The wind cannot make a road
   so it invites the water.
The water creates a road,
The worm follows it and emerges from the ground.
Outside, the worm is so happy.
It has the sky and the fields,
The worm is thrilled,
It feels the whole world is his,
Above the ground,
   it is so much easier to wiggle and move.
The sunlight arrives and visits the worm.
The worm has a nice warm feeling.
After a while its skin feels burned,
The worm wants to return to the ground.
The sunlight made the ground hot with fever,
The worm cannot reach inside the ground,

it is too hot.
It is too hard for the worm to move,
    its skin is burned all over.
The worm's skin turns black,
    just like dirt.

The Sky and Earth

The sky borrows from our planet and the universe.
Our planet borrows from the sky and the stars.
The sky, the earth and the stars
    cannot leave each other because they owe
    and haven't paid back.
Trillions of years pass,
    they cannot pay back what they owe.
How can it be made clear?
Life and death cannot help.
The moment grabs a sword,
It cuts through the loans
    between the sky, the earth and the stars,
Moment by moment, continuously.

Meditation

Meditation follows everything.
After meditation is getting enlightenment,
After enlightenment you still owe.
Finally you understand that owing something
    is more dangerous than getting enlightenment,
You are scared.
That is not a mistake of the sky or earth,
Don't complain about that.
Borrowing never stops, it keeps on going.
The light doesn't understand itself,
The light doesn't understand what owing means,
Borrowing doesn't have a face.
The light squeezes the necks of everyone who owes.

The Colors

The colors of the mind, thinking and action
    all borrow from each other.
You can talk, you can listen,
That is loaning to each other.
Some minds are smart,
    they look for the inside mind,
Finding the inside mind makes them free,
That makes wisdom.
Inside wisdom, the borrower's face cannot appear.
The mind understands that that is all thinking.
Take all thoughts from inside the mind,
Give them freedom.

What Do You Owe?

If you don't borrow air
You cannot breath, you cannot see,
    you cannot listen, you cannot eat.
If you don't want to borrow air,
    then you have to die.
Before you die, you look for heaven.
In heaven, everything owes each other, too.
Where is there no borrowing?
Think about that.
Thinking borrows from the mind too.
Cut every thought and throw them all away,
Become empty.
The emptiness also borrows,
Everything in the universe argues
    about borrowing and not paying back,
Wherever you go, the borrowing is so noisy.

The Moment

You look at each other's face,
That is borrowing,
You talk and listen to each other,
That is also borrowing.
During their lifetime, each person borrows
    an amount that is ten times bigger
    than the universe.
Look inside your mind.
What did you hear, what did you see,
    what knowledge did you get,
    what did you eat, what did you breathe,
    where did you walk, what did you touch?
If you add that up,
    that is ten times bigger than the universe.
Think about the universe, one time,
    and immediately the universe
    is inside your mind.
What you owe is so great,
    how can you pay it all back?
At that moment, moment by moment,
    the moments chase each other,
They look for what they owe.

Inside the Loan

Life begins inside the loan,
Life lives inside the loan,
Life dies inside the loan.
Life and death owe the biggest loan.
Every life comes and goes inside the loan.
The lives don't understand they are inside a loan,
The loan asks them to pay back.
Those who are alive, those who are dead,
The loan chases them forever.

Do You Understand Winter?

Do you understand winter?
The water jumps and runs to the ice
    and closes its eyes.
Winter is so thirsty, it wants to drink water,
The water is frozen, it cannot be drunk.
Winter understands that it made a mistake.
The white snow makes soft wind,
The wind's soft movement makes winter sleep.
Winter dreams,
In the dream, the spring flower's perfume appears.
Winter is shocked,
It wakes up,
Winter wants to run away,
It looks for the road everywhere -
    East, West, South and North.
Winter wants to hide, its time is lost.
Winter is so exhausted,
Spring invites the rain,
Spring washes winter away.

The Winter, the Mountain and the Sky

Winter grabs the mountain and the sky,
It freezes, kicks, punches and gives colds and flus.
Every life almost dies.
Every life gets stronger again.
Winter looks at the lives and is shocked.
Winter looks for the way to return.
Winter forgets how to go back
   to where it came from.
Winter opens its eyes and ears,
   looking and listening everywhere.
Winter finds a leftover piece of ice.
Winter grabs the ice
   and runs to the Himalayan Mountains.
The Himalayan Mountains collect winter
   from everywhere,
The Himalayan Mountains buries winter's face
   in the snow.

The Winter Air Is So Cold

Winter's cold air gives the stream a cold.
Winter's cold air gives the river the flu.
Winter's cold air makes the ocean sneeze.
The stream, river, and ocean water
    have a hard time all winter.
They talk about their experiences,
Their stories are brought out in the
    Spring, Summer, and Fall.
The Spring, the Summer, and the Fall are so noisy.

What is Winter's Greatness?

Winter questions, "What is great about Winter?"
The ice says, "I am great!"
The snow says, "I am great!"
The cold wind says, "I am great!"
Winter looks at them and calls them together,
"Ice, snow and cold air, if one of you is gone,
    it isn't winter anymore. You three are brothers,
    you must help each other.
    That makes Winter great."
The ice understands, the snow understands
    and the cold wind understands,
Together they open their eyes,
Together they open their ears,
And make a celebration.
The Winter is so cold.

What is Winter?

Winter doesn't understand Winter.
Winter visits the ice,
Winter visits the snow,
Winter visits the cold air,
Winter is so busy.
Still, Winter doesn't understand itself.
Winter is very angry.
That makes the mountain and river freeze,
It is even hard for the trees to breath.
Winter sits on the tree and asks,
"Why don't you have any leaves?"
The tree tells Winter,
"Before you came, the Fall took away all the leaves."
Winter understands that it is one step later than Fall.
Winter is ashamed of itself,
	it shakes the tree's branches.
All Winter,
	Winter waits for someone to call its name.
The trees branches call: "Winter!"
Winter listens and is so excited
	to finally understand its name.
Winter asks the ice, the snow and the cold wind
	to bring music for a celebration.
Winter dances on the tree tops.

On the Table

The cup sits on the dining table,
Its mouth is always open.
The cup never says "No" to anything
    that comes to its mouth,
That is the beauty of the cup.
The cup has only one ear.
If a person grabs the cup's ear,
The cup can hear their heartbeat
People don't understand that the cup's ear
    is a stethoscope,
When sickness comes through,
    people always look for a doctor,
Nobody asks the cup how a person's health is,
That always makes the cup sad.

The Cup Never Made Its Name

The cup never made its name
People looked at the cup and called it, 'cup'.
The cup heard itself called 'cup' one time,
    and never forgot its name.
The cup calls itself, 'cup, cup, cup, cup',
    24 hours a day.
People are smart,
They see a cup and understand that it is a cup.
A person grabs the cup
Inside the hand the cup calls itself,
    'cup, cup, cup, cup',
The palm's heart beats,
    'cup, cup, cup, cup'.

The Cup and the Baby

The baby holds the cup and tumbles,
The cup holds the baby and also tumbles,
Day by day, continuously.
The baby grows up and becomes big,
The size of the cup never changes.
The cup never complains.
Why doesn't the cup complain?
Look inside the cup,
All the baby's stories are holding on,
The cup's light is so enormous.

The Cup and the Flower

On the dining room table,
The cup looks at the flower.
The cup moves very carefully,
    closer and closer to the flower,
The cup looks at the flower,
    it is so beautiful, so lovely,
The cup thinks about kissing the flower
    and teasing it.
The flower also thinks about trying to kiss the cup,
The flower is frustrated,
    it becomes so thirsty, it cannot wait;
Finally the flower jumps into the cup's water.
The flower and the cup meet each other
    and they kiss,
That makes a big event.
All the cups on the other table watch,
They are so happy they clap their hands for them.
The people hear the clapping and wake up.
The people go to see the cup,
The flower is inside the cup,
The people pick up the cup and the flower
    and dump them into the sink.
The other cups watch and are shocked.
They see that the people's conduct is very cold.
The cups read the people's minds
    and worry about their future.

One Cup of Coffee

In front of the cup of coffee, a person worries,
The cup worries about the same thing.
In the cup, the coffee is exhausted,
It only makes steam.
Finally, a great idea appears to the person,
And they are happy.
The person grabs the cup of coffee
    and takes one sip.
The cup kisses the person and is elated.
The cup dribbles one drop of coffee
    over the person's lip,
One drop of coffee slides down the chin,
That drop is very excited.

One Family is Sad

One family has no food, they are so hungry.
The father's face is so cloudy,
The mother looks at the fathers face and suffers.
In front of their children,
    they completely have no strength.
They have no food, they don't eat.
They look at each other,
They don't have the energy to hate their hunger,
Their faces completely have no energy,
When can they smile?
The room is so cold,
There is nothing in the kitchen,
Where is a helping hand?
The day asks if help is alive,
The day is afraid to open tomorrow.

Suddenly Sadness Appears

A couple loves strongly,
Suddenly one dies,
That sadness is so strong.
The one who remains cannot even talk.
They look down at the land and up to the sky.
They cannot resolve their sadness.
The couple believed that love was forever,
Where did the truth go?
Where is its tail?
The person is so lonely,
They loved their partner so strongly,
They call their lover's name,
Their lover never answers.
The sadness pushes the person's heart,
The moment comes through the chest,
   and sees the sadness there
The moment doesn't know what to do,
It very carefully runs away.
They lost their love,
When will the sadness heal?
Happiness is waiting for that person,
Happiness didn't expect sadness to be so deep,
Why is sadness so strong?
The person still didn't wake up yet.

Suddenly

Suddenly, parents lose their only child,
  in a car accident.
The hearts of the child's mother and father
  are destroyed, they are in so much pain.
They loved their child so strongly, strongly, strongly.
The child is gone,
The child's future is gone,
They look at the blue sky,
They hit the ground,
Sorrowful sounds emerge,
They cry and cry,
They are in such pain.
Still the child never answers.
Day and night the child's parents only think
  about their lost child,
They cannot forget.
Sometimes they sit down,
  and there is no consciousness inside their bodies.
They only think about
  how much they love their child.
The memories of their child run inside their hearts,
They pray for their child in heaven,
They cry, their tears are so hot,
Inside their tears, their child is crying with them.
The parents never forget that point.

The Desert

The desert sand hides the memories
    of the previous desert.
Those memories are very difficult.
Sometimes the desert sand takes out a memory
    and looks at it.
The sandstorm is jealous of the memories.
The sandstorm wants to know more
    about the memories.
The sandstorm is crazy about the memories,
The sandstorm completely picks the desert up
    and drops it.
The desert sand is so frustrated,
It shakes with worry.

The Desert, the River and the Ocean

The river and the ocean cannot do anything
    about the desert.
The river and the ocean lie beyond the desert,
They want to know the desert's dreams.
The river and the ocean make a cloud,
The cloud becomes a carriage,
That carriage visits the desert, bringing a rain storm.
The rain storm collects the desert's secrets.
The river water's mirror
    and the ocean water's mirror chase each other,
Each wanting to be first.
The blue sky watches and laughs.
The desert looks at the river water's mirror
    and the ocean water's mirror,
        and is shocked.

The Kitchen Makes Dream Sounds

In the kitchen at night, the knife, the bowls,
    the plates and the cups dream.
Nobody knows about that.
The soy sauce and the salt know what is going on.
The soy sauce and the salt wait for the morning
    when everything wakes up.
Then the soy sauce and the salt can pick up
    exactly what the knife, the bowls,
    the plates and the cups were dreaming.
They cannot wait for morning's brightness.

The Truthful Trees

Every kind of difficulty comes to the trees.
The trees pass through,
The trees never brag about themselves,
The trees look beautiful.
The birds come and visit the trees,
The birds always enjoy the trees.
The birds always get what they want from the trees.
The birds sing,
Their songs are truthful.
From the trees,
    the mountain and the river are reborn.

The Truthful Eggs

The eggs are truthful.
The eggs make great lives.
The embryos look for the truthful way.
Finally the baby birds are born.
They open their eyes and look at everything,
It is all so beautiful.
They fly around – East, West, South and North.
The dirt looks at the graceful birds,
The dirt hangs onto the birds' toes and shouts,
"This is truthful! This is graceful!"

The Graceful Animals

The animals are graceful.
They have strong rules,
They never lie to each other,
They never gossip about each other,
They never complain about each other.
Millions and millions of years pass,
They never change those rules.
The animals' history never changes,
They don't need a pen or brush,
The pen and brush never look at them.

The Truthful Mountain

The mountain is graceful.
All of nature's life begins
    on the face of the mountain.
They bring their own dreams,
The dreams grow up and return
    to where they came from.
The truthful mountain introduces
    what is life and what is death.
The mountain's big chest holds onto the truth
    and stands up straight.
The lightning comes and bows
    to the truthful mountain.

The Bell is Truthful

The bell's sound appears, truthfully,
The sky and earth listen to the sound of the bell,
They love the bell's sound.
The truthful bell sound teaches about love
    to every individual person.
People's compassion comes from
    the truthful bell sound.
The truthful bell sound makes
    those in the neighborhood
    understand each other.
The bell's truthful sound goes straight,
    it never stops.

Don't Look Far For Buddha's Mind

You sit down,
You look at Buddha's statue in front of you.
In your eye, Buddha's statue cannot do anything,
It cannot move.
Where is Buddha's mind?
You look, you are so frustrated.
Your thinking looks for Buddha's Mind everywhere,
    day and night.
Finally you are hungry and thirsty.
You run, grab water and drink it,
You grab food and eat it.
Your throat and stomach are reborn again,
Buddha did the same as you,
When he was thirsty, he drank,
When he was hungry he ate.
During his lifetime, his mind practiced that way.
Don't look for Buddha's mind far away,
Look at yourself, look at what you do.

Brand New

The day is brand new,
The face is brand new,
Talking is brand new,
Writing is brand new,
The drawing is brand new,
Everything is brand new.
That is great!
In a moment, a moment runs in
    and 'brand new' is a memory.
The moment washes out the memory's dirt.
The memory's dirt drops, like a sauna.
The moment doesn't look back,
    it keeps going forward.

At the Desk

Someone sits at the desk, studying.
Their mind and their thinking like and dislike.
They push forward and back.
The study book and the note book
    are very angry about that.
The pen grabs cold and hot water
    and throws them at the person studying.
The desk doesn't answer,
    it doesn't complain,
The desk legs are confused.

Hello

You can say, "Hello".
Your mind and thinking are clear,
Your action is correct,
Your body is wonderful,
Nobody can complain.
You look at each other,
You like each other.
Day by day, keep going that way,
That is truth.
Your heart is great,
It holds onto the four seasons, truthfully.
The thunder and lightning try to learn from you,
That makes the clouds so noisy.

The Big Mountain

The big mountain brags.
The grass and trees clap their hands.
The stones invite the clouds to dance.
Nobody pays attention
    to the flying and tumbling dust.
The dust is unhappy.
All the dust gathers,
It picks up and carries the big mountain,
    the grass, the trees and the stones,
One by one, the dust covers them up.
Now, they all understand
    the dust's great and powerful energy,
Finally, they want to learn from the dust.
They give themselves up and open their eyes.
The dust calls the wind.
As it rides away, the dust says,
"Dust is so small, but don't think about
    looking down at the dust, again."
The dust speaks;
The big mountain, the grass, the trees
    and the stones cannot open their mouths,
They cannot count how long they live that way.

The Earthquake

The earthquake appears,
Everything is chaos.
At that moment those who live
    look for those who have died.
The dead cannot say a word,
Their spoken words have gone into the ground.
Everywhere, there is crying.
Even those who don't cry outwardly
    are crying inside their hearts.
This is all more than suffering.
The tears of those who are looking for the dead
    are like a bottomless well.
The crying sound rips through the blue sky.
Everyone wonders, "Why did this happen?"
Their hearts tear out the heart of the earthquake.

The Face of the Earthquake

The earthquake's face is not only inside the ground.
The earthquake's face is inside the cloud,
That makes the lightning wakeup.
The earthquake energy is buried inside people,
That makes people always angry and hateful.
The earthquake energy is inside animals,
It comes through their horns, fangs and claws,
    sharp and bright.
The earthquake looks for a place it doesn't know,
The earthquake looks for a mirror.

The Action is Bright

Your action is bright.
Jealousy and deceit cannot hurt you.
Your action looks forward, clearly.
You want something,
That makes a bridge for you.
Coming and going, everything is great.
The stream water respects that,
It makes itself into a mirror and runs to you.

Bad Action

You do bad action,
Demons, monsters, ghosts, and the devil
   open the door to hell,
The want to show you what really bad action is.
They grab a metal stick and beat you up,
Molten metal dances around you.
They destroy you,
They want to eat you,
They want to satiate their hunger.

The Stream and the Mountain

The stream cuts through the mountain,
Its action is clear.
The mountain cannot copy the stream,
The stream controls the mountain, nicely.
The stream feeds the animals and birds
    and makes them grow,
That is great.
The big stone shows its face in front of the stream,
The stone invites the trees and the flowers
    to dance in celebration,
The stream flows, flows, flows
    and claps its hands for them,
The mountain wakes up again.

The Grass and Trees

The grass and trees dig into the ground,
The grass and trees look good.
The snow and rain come through,
Sometimes, the grass and trees have difficulties,
The grass and trees grow up.
They are so impressive, they are so beautiful,
They make the mountain wealthy,
They never say they are great.
The snow and rain understand
    that the grass and trees are great,
They help them wash their faces.
The wind flies in and help the grass and trees
    to dance.
The birds fly in and talk and sing,
The grass and trees know how to open their ears.
People visit and look at the grass and the trees,
The grass and the trees
    open the people's eyes and ears, brightly.

Water and the Numbers

Water carries the numbers.
The fish look for the numbers, they swim.
The fish open their mouths and close them.
That is how they count,
That is what water is about,
That gives water life.
The fish love the water's numbers.
The fish follow the water's numbers.
The numbers open the day and night.
The numbers make a mirror,
The blue sky jumps into the water,
The blue sky can't move.
The water's numbers flow across the blue sky's face.

The Tiger and the Numbers

The tiger runs over the mountains
    and through the fields.
The tiger's paws make numbers.
While the tiger runs, the grass lays down before it,
That is the grass' wisdom.
The tiger runs away and leaves its footprints behind.
The grass' eyes open and its faces appear.
That is the grass' numbers.
The grass collects the tiger's footprint numbers,
They look for how old the tiger is.

Step By Step

One step, two steps, keep going,
Thinking follows - flowing,
The arms swing,
In the palms, the mind makes a mirror.
The eye's light looks from one thing to another.
East, West, South and North open their doors,
They don't complain.
One day of life continues, step by step
That is great,
In the sky and earth,
Life is breathing.